THE WAY WE DANCED

1949-1999

By EUGÉNIE R. ROCHEROLLE

In Memory of Juliet Shaw

Commissioned by the Duo-Piano Group of the Darien Community Association, Darien, CT,
in Honor of Its 50th Anniversary, May 1999

Editor: DALE TUCKER

CONTENTS

JITTERBUG!

EUGÉNIE ROCHEROLLE

6

PAM0106

10

PAM0106

SLOW DANCIN'

'50s Style

EUGÉNIE ROCHEROLLE

16

18

PAM0106

A WINSOME WALTZ

Eugénie Rocherolle

PAM0106

26

PAM0106

TANGO FOR TWO

EUGÉNIE ROCHEROLLE

"CLASSIC" ROCK

EUGÉNIE ROCHEROLLE

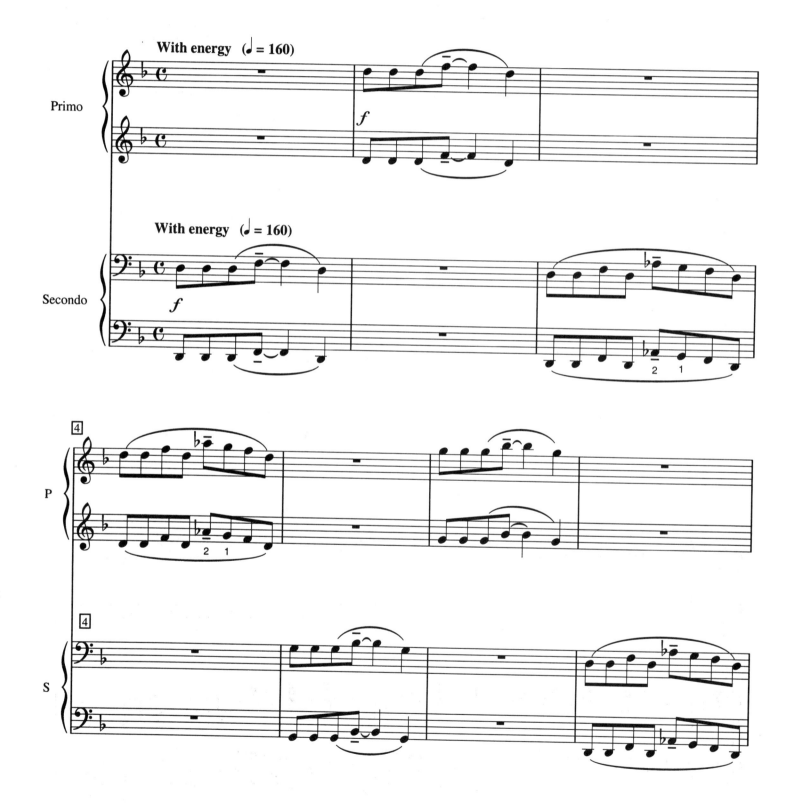

PAM0106

poco rit. on repeat (2nd time to p. 42)

poco rit. on repeat (2nd time to p. 42)

ped. simile

40

PAM0106

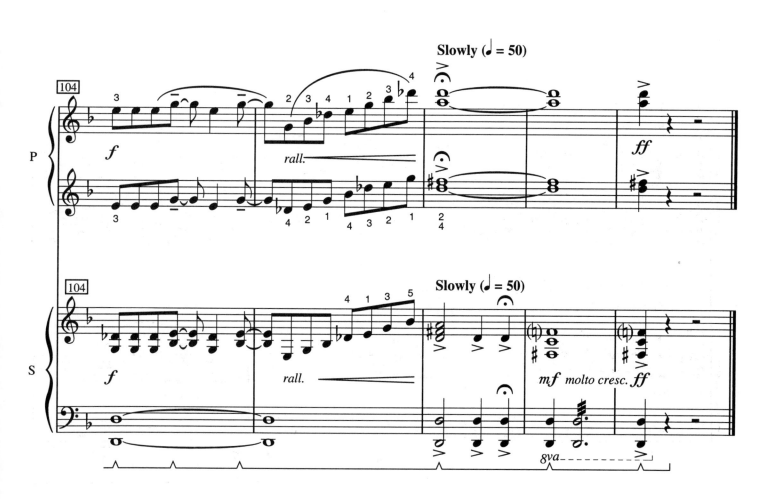

Eugénie Rocherolle

Composer, lyricist, pianist, and teacher, Eugénie Rocherolle began an early publishing career in choral and band music. In 1978, with the success of her first piano solo collection, she soon established herself as one of the leading American composers of piano repertoire. Her music is widely distributed throughout the United States and abroad.

A native of New Orleans, she graduated from Newcomb College of Tulane University with a BA in music. Her junior year was spent in Paris where she had a class with the late Nadia Boulanger. She was honored as the 1995 outstanding Newcomb alumna.

A "Commissioned by Clavier" composer, she was also one of seven composer members of the National League of American Pen Women whose works were chosen to be presented in a concert at the Terrace Theater in the Kennedy Center. Awards from the Pen Women include a first place for both piano and choral in biennial national competitions.

Mrs. Rocherolle's creative output also includes unpublished works in solo voice, chorus, and orchestra; musical theater; and chamber music for a variety of mediums. She is a member of the American Society of Composers, Authors and Publishers (ASCAP); Connecticut Composers Inc.; and the National Federation of Music Clubs. Her biographical profile appears in the *International Who's Who in Music, Baker's Biographical Dictionary of 20th Century Classical Musicians, International Encyclopedia of Women Composers, Who's Who of American Women,* and *Who's Who in the East.*

Mrs. Rocherolle has released recordings of her piano music, *Spinning Gold* and *Romancing the Piano,* and her Christmas arrangements, *Tidings of Joy,* on an independent label, Aureus Recordings.

Mrs. Rocherolle maintains a private studio where she teaches piano and composition.